SUPER QUIBUSDAM

A letter to Mekhitar I of Cilicia, Catholicos of Armenia

Clement VI,
Pope of Rome

Translated by: D.P. Curtin

Dalcassian
Publishing
Company
PHILADELPHIA, PA

Copyright @ 2010 Dalcassian Publishing Company

All rights reserved. No part of this publication may be reproduced, distributed, or transmitted in any form or by any means, including photocopying, recording, or other electronic or mechanical methods, without the prior written permission of the publisher, except in the case of brief quotations embodied in critical reviews and certain other non-commercial uses permitted by copyright law. For permission request, write to Dalcassian Publishing Company at dalcassianpublishing at gmail.com

ISBN: 979-8-8691-7186-3 (Paperback)

Library of Congress Control Number:
Author: Curtin, D.P. (1985-)

Printed by Ingram Content Group, 1 Ingram Blvd, La Vergne, Tennessee

First printing edition 2010.

SUPER QUIBUSDAM

Մխիթար Ա. Գոներցի

SUPER QUIBUSDAM

Sept. 29, 1351

A fuller and clearer profession of faith is demanded of the Armenians.

To my brother the Consolator, the so-called Catholicos of the Armenians, greetings, et cetera.

Upon certain chapters, which for the fuller learning of you and the church of the Armenians in the right and true faith of the Holy Roman and Universal Church, which ruled and reigns with the favor of the Lord who founded it, and who prayed that his faith should not fail, has entered and is treading the unpolluted path along the path of truth , not long ago our brother John, archbishop of Pisa, then Elected of Coron, and Anthony, of good memory, bishop of Gaietan, whom we sent to the parts themselves, entrusting them with the office of full embassage, and for this reason we sent your answers and those of the Church of Armenia Minor, through the same archbishop John, to the aforesaid bishop Anthony in his own prosecution of the journey, at the command of God, and having cleared the debt of nature, we received them under certain chapters, and over them with Ven. to our brethren the Cardinals of the Holy Roman Church and some patriarchs, archbishops and bishops and other ecclesiastical prelates and teachers of sacred theology and teachers of decrees, we could not and cannot elicit from answers like this as to more things, what you and the same Church Minor of Armenia sincerely and purely believe and even if you hold - And therefore, because the simple confession of the holy and catholic faith must be clear, as our Savior and Redeemer teaching us: *he who does -* says (John 3, 20-21) *- the truth, comes to the light, so that his works may be manifested, because in God they were made;* and on the contrary: *He who does evil hates the light and does not come to the light so that his works may be made manifest* . let us fulfill the debt, from some of the answers of yours and of the same Church Minor of Armenia, from some of which are conditioned, from some of which are diminished or incomplete and from some, perhaps due to the fault of the writer or the translator, a less true confession is evidently gathered, we have provided questions to be healthily connected, so that you and the same The Church of Armenia, not in darkness, but in light, responding to them purely and simply, children of light, of that light of truth from the light, which unfailingly persevering *illuminates every person who comes into this world* to be able to enjoy a happy vision in the land of eternal bliss.

1. Therefore, *in the first* chapter *of* your answer, in which you set forth as the foundation of the Catholic faith itself, which you and the Armenian Church, which obeys you, believe and hold, you promise to hold and say that you and the whole Armenian Church obeying you, that the same Roman Church, whose the supreme pontiff is the Roman pope, it is the only Catholic one and in it alone there is true salvation and one true faith and one true Baptism and the true remission of sins, - we ask *first*, if you believe and the Armenian Church which obeys you, all those who in Baptism the same have they received the Catholic faith and subsequently withdrawn from the communion of the faith of the same Roman Church, which is the only Catholic one, or will they withdraw in the future, being schismatics and heretics, if they persist in being persistently divided from the faith of the Roman Church itself? - *Secondly*, we ask, if you believe that you and the Armenians obeying you, that no traveler can be finally saved outside the faith of the Church itself and the obedience of the Roman Pontiff?

II. But *in the second chapter* you say that you believe and hold that the Roman Pontiff alone has the fullness of power which the blessed Peter the Apostle had and that the Roman Pontiff alone is the universal Vicar of Christ. and that you are the Catholicon of the Armenians and must be obedient to the Roman Pontiff, yet because of this obedience you do not wish to diminish yourself or your Church in any way, nor to destroy nor diminish the graces, liberties, cares, dioceses, rights and power to command all the Armenians, which your predecessors and the Church Armenians received and held by the Roman Church itself, nay, you beseech that for you and your Church, remaining aforesaid, we, who are the Roman Pontiff, increase the liberties and rights of you and your Church as much as is possible according to God, to our everlasting memory.

Again, you say that you believe and maintain that the Antiquities of the Catholic and Apostolic Church must be obedient to the Roman Pontiff, because Christ gave the fullness of power to blessed Peter for himself and for his lieutenants.

Likewise, you say that you believe that every Roman Pontiff, who is supreme, past, present and future, was, is and will be the lieutenant of blessed Peter, because he was and is and will be immediately the universal Vicar of Christ.

Again, you promise that, as much as it will be in you, you will see to it that all your subjects, ecclesiastical and secular, firmly believe and hold all the aforesaid things.

Therefore we complain *first of all about these:* if you have believed, believe or are ready to believe with the Armenian Church which obeys you, that blessed Peter received the most complete power of jurisdiction over all faithful Christians from the Lord Jesus Christ and that all the power of jurisdiction, as in certain countries and provinces and different in the parts of the world Judas Thaddeus and the other apostles had a special and particular authority, it was subject to the most complete authority and power, which over all who believe in Christ in all parts of the world the blessed Peter received from the Lord Jesus Christ himself, and that no apostle or anyone else over all Christians, except Peter alone received full power?

Second : if you have believed, held, or are ready to believe and hold with the Armenians who are subject to you, that all the Roman Pontiffs who succeeded the blessed Peter canonically entered and will enter canonically, they themselves succeeded the blessed Peter the Roman Pontiff and will succeed in the same full jurisdiction of power as the blessed Petras himself did he receive from the Lord Jesus Christ over the entire body of the Church militant?

Thirdly: if you believed and believe you and the Armenians subject to you, the Roman Pontiffs who have been and We who are the Roman Pontiff and those who will successively be in the future, as legitimate and full of power Vicars of

Christ all the powerful jurisdiction that Christ as Head had conformably in human life, that he received directly from Christ himself over the entire and universal Body of the militant Church?

Fourthly: if you believed and believe that all the Roman Pontiffs who have been, we who are and others who will be in the future, could, can and will be able directly through us and them over everything as our jurisdiction and their subjects to judge, and to judge whomsoever we will appoint and delegate ecclesiastical judges?

Fifthly: if you have believed and believe that it has been, and will be, the supreme and pre-eminent authority and juridical power of the Roman Pontiffs who have been, of us who are and of those who will be in posterity, so that they could not be judged by anyone, we could and they will not be able to posterity, but God alone has been saved from judging, we will be saved and they will be saved, and that from Our judgments and judgments he could not, and cannot, and will not be able to appeal to any other judge?

Sixth: If you believed and still believe that the full power of the Roman Pontiff extends to such an extent that patriarchs, catholicons, archbishops, bishops, abbots and any other prelates from the positions in which they have been appointed can transfer to other positions of greater or lesser jurisdiction, or at their request crimes, to degrade and depose them, to excommunicate them, and to hand them over to Satan?

Seventh: if you believed, and still believe, that pontifical authority cannot and should not be subject to any imperial or royal or other secular power, as far as judicial appointment, correction or dismissal?

Eighth: if you believed and believe that the Roman Pontiff can establish sacred general canons, to grant the fullest indulgence to those who visit the thresholds of the Apostles Peter and Paul, or those approaching the Holy Land, or to any faithful who truly and fully repent and confess?

Ninth: if you believed and do believe, that all those who raised themselves against the faith of the Roman Church and died in final impenitence, were damned and descended to the eternal torments of hell?

Tenth: if you believed and still believe, the Roman Pontiff regarding the administration of the Sacraments of the Church, always saving what concerns the integrity and necessity of the Sacraments, could he tolerate the different rites of the Churches of Christ and even allow them to be observed?

Eleventh: if you believed and do you believe that the Armenians, who obey the Roman Pontiff in different parts of the world and observe the forms and rites of the Roman Church in the administration of the Sacraments and in ecclesiastical offices, fasts and other ceremonies, diligently and with devotion, do well and by doing so earn eternal life?

Twelfth: if you believed and still believe that no one can be transferred from episcopal dignity to archbishopric, patriarchal or catholic by his own authority, nor even by the authority of any secular prince, be it king or emperor or anyone else, supported by any earthly power and dignity?

Thirteenth: if you have believed and still believe, only the Roman Pontiff, with doubts arising about the Catholic faith, can, through an authentic determination, to which he must inviolably adhere, put an end to being true and Catholic, whatever he himself determines to be true by the authority of the keys handed down to him by Christ; and what determines that it is false and heretical, is it to be considered?

Fourteenth: if you have believed and believe that the New and Old Testaments in all the books which the authority of the Roman Church has handed down to us, contain the undoubted truth in everything?

In answer to the articles sent by us also of the Minor Church of Armenia, you presuppose that what you are going to say is about the doctrine of the Old and

New Testaments, Thaddeus and Bartholomew the Apostles and the universal council of the Holy, Catholic and Apostolic Church handed down to be believed and held by the Armenian Church *and so on.*

Upon which we ask of you the following:

First: if you believed that the doctrine of the New and Old Testament was issued by the blessed Apostles Thaddeus and Bartholomew or was revealed only to those preachers of the Catholic Church through them?

Secondly: if you believed and believe that Thaddeus was presiding over Judas and Bartholomew, Andrew, James the Greater and the Lesser, John the Evangelist and the rest of the Apostles from Peter, or was he of greater authority?

In the second chapter you write that you and the Armenians obeying you should believe that the Holy Spirit proceeds from the Father and the Son, and that until now you and the Armenians obeying you in particular have said, but from now on, as far as you can, you will say this generally. - In regard to that chapter we would like you to answer the following questions:

First: if you have believed and held that it is necessary for salvation to believe that the Holy Spirit proceeds not from the Father alone, but also from the Son from eternity?

Secondly: if you considered those who expressly denied that the Holy Spirit proceeds from the Son to be schismatics and heretics, do you still have and will you always in the future?

Thirdly: if in the office of the Mass, on the days when, according to the custom of the Roman Church, the first Symbol is sung, are you ready and willing to sing and confess before the people that the Holy Spirit proceeds from the Father and the Son, as contained in the said Symbol?

Fourthly: if you believed and believe that the Holy Spirit proceeds from the Father and the Son as from one beginning through one breath, existing in common with the Father and the Son, as the general council of the Roman Church and the Catholic Doctors, whom the same Church venerates as saints, teach?

Fifthly: if you have believed and believe that the Holy Spirit is one God with the Father and the Son and is equal to them in all things, in power, in will, in immensity to him in all matters; not in a lower degree or later in time, but eternally with the same eternity?

Sixth: because you write that until now you have said specifically that the Holy Spirit proceeds from the Father and the Son, but from now on, as far as you can, you will say generally. We ask of you, if you understand by *private* what you said privately and not in public, or that some of the Armenians, though private and few, believed and said that the Holy Spirit proceeds from the Father and the Son? *In general* , however, the community of Armenia Minor did not believe or say that the Holy Spirit would proceed from the Son, nor does it seem ready to say so easily. because you write that as much as you can do, it should be said *generally* .

In the second chapter you write that you should believe and hold that in one single person of Christ there are two natures, that is to say human and divine, united. - Upon which we would like to know, if you believe or are ready to believe, you and the Armenians who obey you, that in Christ the only eternal person of the Son of God, in two perfect and whole natures, indeed the divine which he had eternally and the human, which from the time of the blessed virgin's womb Did he take Mary as his mother?

Secondly: if you consider all those heretics who believe and believe in the future, that in Christ there remains only one nature, just as there is only one person in him, and if you and the Armenians who obey you detest Eutyches and Dioscorus and the rest of their heretical accomplices . , do you firmly believe that the divine essence among the Saints can be clearly seen and blissfully enjoyed by others?

Thirdly: if you believed, or are you prepared to believe, that the Antiochian bishop Macharius and his accomplices, who were building a single will and action in Christ, were justly and catholically condemned and anathematized by the Roman Pontiff Agathon in the sixth Constantinople Synod with their heresies?

Fourthly: if you believed and believe, you and the Armenians who obey you, Vartan, whom, as it has been reported and asserted to us by many, the Armenians had as a special teacher and who infected many of Armenia Minor with heresy, teaching and writing that the Holy Spirit does not proceed from the Son, but from the Father alone, and that Christ has only one nature, and that Christ himself did not give greater authority to Peter than to the other apostles, and that the Roman Church has no jurisdiction or any power over the Church of the Armenians, and that the spirits of all men were at the same time created by God, and that souls to be saved and damned remain outside Paradise and Hell until the day of judgment, and holy souls will not see God in His essence as a beatific, nor will they enjoy it until the day of judgment; nor will those who have departed from their bodies with mortal sin be tormented in Hell until the aforesaid day of the final judgment; and that the Catholic Church must pray for the souls of the Blessed Virgin, the blessed Peter and Paul the Apostles, and all the Saint Martyrs and those who died without any fault whatsoever and without any obligation to the punishments of Purgatory; and that according to humanity Christ is equal to God the Father; so of many other errors, of which there is one great book, which the said Vartan is said to have composed against the holy faith of the Roman Church, scattered throughout, that he was a worst heretic and heresiarch, and he, together with the said heresies and others, in that book or in other writings or doctrines of the same content, in so far as those scriptures, or any of his doctrines or sayings, are contrary to the scriptures and doctrine of the faith of Jesus Christ, which the Roman Church teaches and holds; and all the councils of the Armenians, wherever and by whomsoever, have been assembled against the faith of the

Roman Church and the articles of the Christian faith, which the Roman Church teaches and holds, considering, believing, and holding that they were a congregation of heretics and adversaries of the faith of our Lord Jesus Christ, and if those who taught such things were heretics and do you anathematize their teaching as heretical and detest it as the poison of the faith of Jesus Christ?

III. In *the third chapter* you say that you believe that those who are born and will be born of man and woman contract original sin, in addition to the personal sins which the first parents contracted by eating from the fruit of the forbidden tree commanded against them by the Lord. - About which chapter we want to know from you and from the Armenians who obey you:

First: if you believe that the actual sins of the first parents contracted from them those who were born and those who will be born from them and will contract them in the future, how do they contract the original sin from them?

Secondly: if you believe that original sin is contracted because of all the actual sins of the first parents?

Thirdly: if you believe that circumcision was only performed around the opening of the kingdom of heaven before the institution of Baptism and the obligation to it of all who descend from the first parents in both sexes through propagation, how much does Baptism work from then on?

6. *In the sixth chapter* you say that you believe with the Armenians who obey you, that all the souls of the deceased, completely cleansed of their sins after Christ's passion, immediately go to the kingdom of heaven, where they see God clearly; and the souls of those who die in mortal sin go to Hell of damnation, where they will never see God, but are punished there by sensual combat (yes!). - About what we want to know from you.

First: if you believe or are ready to believe, that after the passion and ascension of the Lord Jesus Christ, the souls of those who died in the grace of Christ and in whom there was nothing to be cleansed when they died, ascended into the kingdom of heaven and the heavenly paradise and gathered with Christ and the company of the holy angels, divine let them see the essence with facial vision as it is, the divine essence itself immediately, clearly and openly showing itself to them?

Secondly, if you have believed, or are ready to believe, that they enjoy the same essence of the soul, having nothing that can be separated from their bodies, and that from the vision and enjoyment of the divine essence they are truly blessed, and that this kind of intuitive and facial clear and open vision and enjoyment in the same souls without any interruption or does it continue to exist and continue until the final judgment and from then on to eternity?

Thirdly: if you believe, or are you ready to believe, that the souls of those who have died in actual mortal sin immediately after their death descend to hell, where they are tormented by infernal punishments without remedy and without extinguishing the fire, with a perpetual punishment of lack of vision and blissful enjoyment?

VII. In *the seventh chapter* you say that you believe with the Armenians who obey you, that true happiness lies in the vision of God and not in the vision of any other thing. - About what we want to know from you:

First: if you have believed and do believe, that true happiness does not consist in seeing God through a mirror in an enigma, but in a vision in which God appears face to face as He is?

Secondly: if you believed and still believe that true happiness is not found without delay corresponding (?) to the facial vision of God?

VIII. About *the eighth chapter* we ask:

First: if you believed and still believe that Christ according to humanity does not exceed in infinite perfection every created creature, nor does the happiness with which his soul is blessed exceed in infinite perfection the happiness of angels or blessed souls?

Secondly: if you have believed and believe, Christ according to humanity, in which he is inferior to the Father, will you exceed infinitely and without limit the perfection which he has according to divinity, in which he is equal to the Father and the Holy Spirit?

X. We ask about *the tenth chapter,* if you have believed and believe that there is Purgatory, to which the souls of those who have died in grace descend, which have not yet satisfied their sins through complete penance? - Also, if you believed and still believe that they will be crucified for a time and that they will soon be cleansed even on this day of judgment and reach true and eternal happiness, which consists in the facial vision and love of God?

In *the twelfth chapter* you say that Baptism, received according to the form of the Church without pretense, wipes out all the sins of those who are once baptized, whether they be original or actual; but when some are baptized twice in the same Baptism, their sins are not blotted out, on the contrary, they are added and committed through the second Baptism. - About that:

First: we want to know from you, if you believe, that Baptism received according to the form of the Roman Church, which is: *I baptize you in the name of the Father and of the Son and of the Holy Spirit,* in those who receive it without feigning or crying, let it destroy all original and actual things, if they are present sins to them?

Secondly: if you believe that the aforesaid form which the Roman Church uses was instituted by Christ and delivered to the Apostles, and that it was imposed by Christ and through the Apostles on the Catholic Church, which is Roman, to be kept?

Thirdly: if you believe that Baptism should be conferred by any mortal man having faith in the Sacrament, not even a priest or cleric, but a layman or a woman, in the form used by the Roman Church, it is true that Baptism is neither knowingly repeated by any minister nor received by him who was he once baptized in the said form of the Roman Church, without mortal sin?

Fourthly, if you believe, supposing that it were lawful to interpose the gospel or some prayers between the utterance of the words of the form of Baptism and the anointing with baptismal water, that it would be much better and more orderly if, when the words of Baptism are pronounced, the anointing is done at the same time as the baptismal water of the one being baptized?

Fifthly: if you believe that there is no authority to which a Catholic can adhere, or that it can be proved by effective reason, that the form used by the Roman Church in baptizing is doubtful and uncertain, and that the Apostles did not use it when baptizing? - What we want to know from you for so much, because you have sent some weakly concluding reasons, for what you assume as much as possible in all those reasons, which you ought to prove.

Concerning *the 17th chapter,* in which you say that you believe that Marriage is a Sacrament of the Church and that the matrimonial act, if performed in an appropriate manner, is meritorious, we would like to know from you if you believe that the Sacrament of Matrimony, perfect and consummated by carnal union, cannot in any way be dissolved as far as the bond is otherwise than by the death of the other spouse or of both, saying to the Lord: *What God has joined together, shall not man separate? Secondly:* if you believe that a dead wife, who was her husband, can marry a second wife and, when she is dead, a third wife, and so on, as long as it pleases him and he is fit for marriage; and that in a similar manner a wife may marry a second time to her first dead husband, and likewise to a third dead husband, and so on to other dead first husbands?

Regarding *the 23rd chapter,* in which you say that you believe that the human nature assumed by the Word is substantially united to the Word in the unity of the person, we ask you if you believe that the unity of human and divine nature in the Word is not substantial, but personal; nor that the divine and human natures are substantially united, but suppositively in the unity of the person?

Regarding *the 24th chapter,* in which you say and promise what you will take care to do, so that your subjects do not receive the laying on of hands except from those who obey you, as you do of the Roman Church, we ask:

First: from you, if you believe that those who obey the Roman Church and you can receive the imposition of hands from the Roman Pontiff or from other bishops under the authority of the Roman Pontiff?

Secondly: if you believe that all who obey you are bound more immediately and principally to obey the Roman Pontiff than you?

About *the 30th and 31st chapters,* in which you say, *first,* that the flesh of animals which are killed for the burial of the dead, to be helped by alms, and that the distinction between clean and unclean animals, as regards eating, which were commanded in the Old Law, ceased and was emptied by the coming of Christ; - we ask you, if you believe that such alms, which are given from meats prohibited by the Law, benefit the souls of the deceased more than if they were given from non-prohibited ones? and how much would they profit them if they had bread, wine, or cloth, or other things, of which the priests and other poor men needed as much or more?

About *the 32nd chapter,* in which you write that it is not the custom of the Armenians to eat fish and oil on fasting days, in fact, by the order of the Armenian Church, it is forbidden to eat fish and oil, and that in praise of those who are satisfied with one meal on fasting days, we ask:

First: from you, if you believe that it is not a commandment of the Catholic Church, that on the days of fasting all those who are fasting should abstain from fish and oil, and that such abstinence is due to the necessity of fasting established by the Holy Fathers?

Secondly: if you believe that those who eat more than once a day violate the fast established by the Roman Church and the Holy Fathers?

In *chapter 39* you say that those duly baptized in the Catholic and Apostolic Church are in no way to be baptized again. What do we ask you about, if by the Catholic and Apostolic Church you understand the Roman Church?

Secondly: if in the Symbol where we have: *into one holy Catholic,* as you also have the Armenians who obey you: *And into this holy Catholic* and if you are prepared to say: *And into one,* as the Roman Church says?

In *the 42nd chapter* you say that you believe and hold that the Body of Christ, born of the Virgin and dead on the Cross, which is now alive in heaven, after the words of the consecration of the bread which are: *This is my body,* it is in the Sacrament of the altar under the form and likeness of bread; from which we ask of you:

First: if you believe that the bread will be transubstantiated into the Body of Christ?

Secondly: if after those words: *This is my body,* the priests in the Armenian Church use prayers, by which they seem to pray, that the bread be turned and passed into the body of Christ, or that it become the body of Christ? and if you and the Armenians who obey you are ready to completely and completely dismiss such prayers, or at least to correct them in so far as they pray for the body of Christ to be on the altar, after the words of consecration truly and truly are the Body of Christ in the Sacrament itself?

Thirdly: we ask you, what words do the Armenian priests use in the consecration of the blood of Jesus Christ?

And for the conclusion of what you have written in the 53rd chapter, we want to know from you if you submit everything written by you to our correction, as the true Vicar of Jesus Christ and the successor of the blessed Peter, the prince of the Apostles, in full authority over all who invoke the name of our Lord Jesus Christ? And to the correction also of our successors and of the Roman Church, which can never fail in believing?

Again, concerning your answers to the instructions given to you and to the Armenians who obey you, through the oft-mentioned John the archbishop and Anthony the bishop, you have given answers which lead *us* to require of you the following:

First: concerning the consecration of Chrism, if you believe that Chrism can be properly and properly consecrated by any priest who is not a bishop?

Secondly: if you believe that the Sacrament of Confirmation cannot be ordinarily administered by someone other than a bishop?

Thirdly: if you believe that only through the Roman Pontiff, who has full power, can the administration of the Sacrament of Confirmation be entrusted to priests who are not bishops?

Fourthly: if you believe that those who are chrismated by any priests who are not bishops, nor have received any commission or concession in this regard from the Roman Pontiff, are they to be chrismated again by a bishop or bishops?

Regarding the second instruction, that the body of Christ should not be given to children when they are baptized, nor should it be placed in their mouths, you answer that it will be given only to those who are baptized in adulthood. - Regarding what answer do we seek, if you believe that before the use of reason the consecrated sacrifice should not be served to anyone?

Secondly: if the adult age, in which no one is fit to receive the Body and Blood of Jesus Christ, do you not believe until he has at least completed the seventh year?

Regarding the fourth instruction, in which the Sacrament of Extreme Anointing is treated, if you believe that every adult mortal man, in the only case where he is gravely infirm and placed in mortal danger, must devoutly and faithfully, once while in the same infirmity, receive the Sacrament of Extreme Anointing require and undertake? that if, not having faith in this Sacrament, he omitted it, or the priest refused to administer it for the same reason, both would sin grievously and err in faith?

Regarding the ninth instruction, which was that Armenians who reasonably doubt whether they were truly baptized in the form in which the Armenians baptize, should not be conditionally forbidden to be baptized according to the form of the Roman Church, you answered that those duly baptized in the Armenian Church, by whomsoever they are baptized, are not to be baptized again in any way; but those who reasonably doubt must refer their doubt to the wise Prelates of the Armenian Church, who, if necessary, will baptize them according to the Armenian form. About which answer:

First: we ask you, in the event that those who were baptized in the form of the Armenians doubted whether they had been baptized or not, and for the doubt to be cut off from their hearts they returned to the Roman Church, if you are prepared to believe that what the Roman Church determined is true?

Secondly, if the Armenians, doubting the form of Baptism in which the Church of the Armenians baptizes, should bring their doubt to the wise Prelates of the Church of the Armenians, we would like to know from you whether they would kindly and charitably receive such and satisfy their doubts by the instruction of the Holy Scriptures, or rather scourge the doubters, imprison them, and would they kill, as it has been reported to us what they did with regard to those Armenians who had been baptized under condition according to the form of the Roman Church by our said messages?

Regarding instruction 11, which is that the Armenians celebrate festivals on the days established by the Roman Church, you answer that the capital festivals are celebrated in the same way as the Roman Church, but other festivals are celebrated according to the Armenian calendar. - Regarding what answer do we seek, if you and your Armenian subjects are ready to celebrate the festivals of the Saints whom the Roman Church honors and venerates everywhere? and if you are prepared to receive the calendar used by the Roman Church, that you may use it in venerating and honoring the Saints whom the Roman Church venerates and honors on the days established for this purpose by the Roman Church?

In the sixteenth instruction you answer that those Saints whom the Catholic and Apostolic Church have already accepted and honored, you and the Armenians have likewise accepted and honored; and the Saints whom the Roman Church accepts and honors, when you accept and honor them, and as for the rest, when you accept and honor them as a saint, you will do so by the will and knowledge of the Roman Church.

First of all, what answer do we want from you, if you believe that the Catholic and Apostolic Church is the same or different from the Roman Church? which is why we are forced to ask, because in the immediately preceding answer, you seem to distinguish the holy Catholic Church from the Roman one, as if you believed that the Roman Church was not Catholic.

Secondly: if you believe that heretics and heresiarchs, as they say were Dioscorus, Eriscartus, James and Rassus, and many others, are not to be honored and venerated as saints by the Catholic Church, but rather to be anathematized and detested?

Regarding instruction 19 concerning the illegitimate, that they should not be promoted to Sacred Orders without the dispensation of the Roman Pontiff, you reply that the Catholicon of the Armenians has hitherto dispensed, and you want the same to be done with the rest, although it is seldom dispensed with such.

In regard to which answer we wish to know from you, when the dispensation of illegitimate children to be promoted to the Holy Orders is a case specially reserved among others to the Roman Pontiff, as you wish, so that other bishops obedient to the Roman Pontiff may not dispense in the aforesaid case without the special privilege and concession of the Roman Pontiff?

Regarding instruction 20, which is about the books used by the Armenian Church, you answer that there are no errors in them, but the praises and glory of God; and in those where it was necessary to correct them, they were corrected.

In regard to what answer we seek from you, why did you not present the books which the Armenian Church uses in the services of the Masses and the hours and the ordinations and consecrations of bishops, nor did you even wish to present them to the interpreter of the aforesaid archbishop and bishop?

Secondly, we would like to know from you if you are faithfully and completely prepared to present them to our messengers, when you were required by them?

Thirdly: You do not answer about the books of those whom you regard as teachers among the Armenians, in which, as has been reported to Us, there are many errors and heresies against the same Catholic faith which the Holy Mother Church holds and teaches. We would like to know from you, then, if you are ready to submit to our order, when it reaches you, books of this kind?

After all that has been said, we are forced to wonder strongly, that in a certain epistle, which begins with *the Honorable Fathers in Christ,* you remove the 16th chapter from the 53 first chapters: *First,* that the Holy Spirit proceeds from the Father and the Son. *Thirdly,* that children contract original sin from their first parents. *Sixthly,* that souls purified from the whole, separated from their bodies, see God clearly. *Ninth,* that the souls of those who die in mortal sin descend into Hell. *Twelfth,* that baptism wipes out original and actual sin. *Of the thirteenth,* which Christ did not destroy by descending to the underworld, the lower Hell. *Fifteenth,* that the angels were created good. *Thirtieth,* that the shedding of the blood of animals does not effect the remission of sins. *The thirty-second*, that they should not judge those who eat fish and oil during fasting days. *The thirty-ninth*, that those who have been baptized in the Catholic Church, if they become infidels and are afterwards converted, are not to be baptized again. *Lent*, that infants may be baptized before the eighth day, and that Baptism cannot be in any liquid other than real water. *Second Lent*, that the body of Christ after the words of consecration is the same number as the body born of the Virgin and sacrificed on the cross. *The fifth Lent*, that no one, not even a Saint, can finish the body of Christ unless he is a priest. *The sixth of Lent*, which is about the need for salvation to confess to one's own priest or with his permission, all mortal sins completely and distinctly.

Therefore, since the words of that letter in which you write, which you reduced to 16 chapters out of 53 chapters presented to you by the said archbishop and bishop, and to each of the answers given by you to them in writing, are complicated and obscure, therefore we want to know clearly and without veiling from you, if the aforesaid Did you reduce the 16 chapters out of the 53 because you do not believe that they are true or Catholic, or for what reason did you reduce the chapters themselves?

Again, in writings you asked the archbishop and the bishop of your ancestors, that there should be an end of words between them and you; and that you no longer labor in words of instruction, for which labor the same archbishop and bishop were sent to you by the Roman See. And since your answers are in most cases dubious, sarcastic, obscure, and suspicious, know that we, who have a burning desire for your safety and that of the Armenians, as we are bound, could not put an end to it, nor cease from labor and fatigue, unless first clearly, clearly, by your obedience you and the Armenians will completely and completely receive that faith which the Roman Church itself holds and teaches, which is the mother and teacher of all the faithful.

Furthermore, since the canonizations of Saints and the promotion of illegitimates to the Sacred Orders are cases which, among others, are reserved only to the Roman Pontiff and do not belong to any other Prelate of the Church, unless the Roman Pontiff himself specifically directs them to be entrusted to certain ones, we are surprised that you say that you want the aforesaid two cases by your own authority to hold you back; that there is no sign of the obedience and reverence which you claim to have towards the Roman Pontiff in the foregoing chapters. Wherefore we are still compelled to require you to answer us in writing, if you wish to reverently accept, teach and keep the traditions of the orthodox Fathers and the Decretals or Constitutions of the holy and apostolic Roman See?

Moreover, because the report of many worthy of the faith, and of some Armenians as well, has often been instilled in our ears, that you and your predecessors, the Catholicos of the Armenians, and the Armenians who obey you and them, have described to us and to our predecessors the Roman Pontiffs, in your letters and theirs, the things concerning the worship of our faith itself. You also promised to do so, but in no way did you fully observe, nay, what is more detestable and We further deplore, the so-called Sees of messengers and envoys, whom the See itself, anxious for your safety and theirs, and anxious for their safety, destined for you and for those Sees, wholesome and sound Catholic doctrine , through the same ambassadors and messengers communicated and delivered to you and your predecessors and those who obeyed you and the same Armenians, you despised and completely rejected and rejected the faith of the Roman Church itself, outside of which there is no grace, no salvation, you held in derision.

And therefore we admonish, require, and exhort your fraternity attentively, exhorting you with sound counsels with a view to your salvation, in so far as to make answers through you to our questions and all that you and the same obeying you, as it is preferred, promise and say to the Armenians about the business of our faith itself, you to believe and hold, although we hope undoubtedly, that your simple words and the pure and true truths of the Armenians themselves and their conscience, whatever he or she tries to assert, will be accompanied by touching the sacred Gospels, strengthened by solemn oaths and nevertheless promised under similar oaths, that to us and to our successors to our Roman Pontiffs canonically entering, and to the same Roman Church and to ours and to their commands and commands, as truly obeying, you will appear with effect, so as to stop the mouths of you and the same Armenians who are so gravely and noticeably obstructing them, and the good shepherd of the clergy and people of Armenia, thus leading them to salvation and prepare pastures, that when the time of resolution arrives, you may enter the holy of holies with purified minds. of the Church, let us gather, it will be known for certain that, in addition to the rewards of eternal salvation and the titles of fame, which you will obtain by providence, God, that most abundant rewarder of all, will give you, so that in the present world also you will flow with graces and favors, and we, although insufficient merits, by his condescension in his Vicar of the lands, who will not detract from the honor and state of the Church and his See, but add to yours, as we hope, by the exacting merits, with the favor of God, we propose to honor you and your Church itself with great and greater privileges, graces and liberties.

Given at Villamnova, in the diocese of Avignon, on the 3rd of October, in the tenth year of our pontificate.

LATIN TEXT

SUPER QUIBUSDAM

ad Mekhitar (=Consolatorem), Catholicon Armeniorum

29 Sept. 1351

Plenior et clarior professio fidei ab Armenis postulatur

Ven. fratri Consolatori, dicto Catholicon Armenorum, salutem etc.

Super quibusdam capitulis, quae pro pleniori eruditione tua et ecclesiae Armenorum in fide recta et vera Sanctae Romanae ac Universalis Ecclesiae, quae favente Domino qui eam fundavit, rexit et regit quique, ut fides eius non deficeret exoravit, per veritatis viam impolluta calle incessit et graditur, dudum per ven. fratrem nostrum Johannem archiepiscopum Pisanum tunc Electum Coronensem et bonae memoriae Antonium episcopum Gaietanum, quos ad partes ipsas, commisso eis in illis plenae legationis officio, signanter propterea misimus, responsiones tuas et Ecclesiae Minoris Armeniae, per eundem Johannem archiepiscopum, praefato Antonio episcopo in sui prosecutione itineris, iubente Deo, naturae debitum exolvente, sub certis capitulis comprehensas, benigne recepimus et super eis cum Ven. fratribus nostris Sanctae Romanae Ecclesiae Cardinalibus ac nonnullis patriarchis, archiepiscopis et episcopis aliisque Praelatis ecclesiasticis ac Sacrae Theologiae magistris et Decretorum doctoribus habita deliberatione matura, non potuimus nec possumus ex responsionibus huiusmodi quoad plura elicere, quid tu et eadem Ecclesia Minoris Armeniae sincere et pure credatis ac etiam teneatis. — Et ideo, quia confessio sanctae et catholicae fidei simplex debet esse clara, sicut Salvator et Redemptor noster nos edocens: *qui facit—* inquit (Io 3, 20-21)*— veritatem, venit ad lucem, ut manifestentur opera eius, quia in Deo facta sunt;* et e contra: *Qui mala agit, odit lucem et non venit ad lucem ut fiant opera eius manifesta,* Nos de tua ceterorumque Armenorum sicut aliorum quoque fidelium, quorum curam providentia Nobis divina commisit, ex paternae charitatis affectu attente solliciti, ut nostrum in hac parte debitum impleamus, quibusdam ex ipsis tuis et eiusdem Ecclesiae Minoris Armeniae responsionibus, ex quarum aliquibus conditionata, ex quibusdam vero diminuta vel imperfecta et ex nonnullis, forsitan scriptoris vel interpretis vitio, minus vera confessio manifeste colligitur, interrogationes providimus salubriter subnectendas, ut tu et eadem Armeniae Ecclesia, non in tenebris, sed in luce, ad illas pure ac simpliciter respondentes, effecti lucis filii, illius luminis veri de lumine, quod indeficiens perseverans *omnem hominem venientem in hunc mundum illuminat* in aeternae beatitudinis patria felici visione perfrui valeatis.

I. *In primo* igitur *capitulo* responsionis tuae, in quo pro fundamento ipsius catholicae fidei praemittis, quod tu et Ecclesia Armenorum, quae tibi oboedit, creditis et tenetis, promittitis tenere et dicitis tu et tota Ecclesia Armenorum tibi oboedientium, quod eadem Ecclesia Romana, cuius summus pontifex est papa Romanus, est sola catholica et in ea sola est vera salus et una vera fides et unum verum Baptisma et vera remissio peccatorum, — querimus *primo,* si creditis tu et Ecclesia Armenorum quae tibi oboedit, omnes illos, qui in Baptismo eandem fidem catholicam receperunt et postmodum a communione fidei eiusdem Ecclesiae Romanae, quae una sola catholica est, recesserunt vel recedent in futurum, esse schismaticos et haereticos, si pertinaciter divisi a fide ipsius Romanae Ecclesiae perseverent? —*Secundo* petimus, si creditis tu et Armeni tibi oboedientes, quod nullus homo viatorum extra fidem ipsius Ecclesiae et oboedientiam Pontificum Romanorum poterit finaliter salvus esse?

II. *In secundo* vero *capitulo* dicis te credere et tenere, quod solus Pontifex Romanus habet plenitudinem potestatis, quam beatas Petrus apostolus habebat et quod ipse Pontifex Romanus solus est universalis Christi Vicarius; et quod tu Catholicon Armenorum es et esse debes oboediens Pontifici Romano, propter hanc tamen oboedientiam non vis te vel tuam Ecclesiam in aliquo minorare nec perdere nec diminuere gratias, libertates, curas, dioceses, iura et potestatem iubendi omnibus Armenis, quae tui praedecessores et Ecclesia Armenorum receperunt et tenuerunt ab ipsa Romana Ecclesia, imo deprecaris, quod tibi et Ecclesiae tuae, praedictis remanentibus, Nos, qui sumus Romanus Pontifex, accrescere faciamus libertates et iura tua et tuae Ecclesiae quantum secundum Deum fieri potest, ad nostri memoriam sempiternam.

Iterum dicis te credere et tenere, quod Antistites de catholica et apostolica Ecclesia debent esse oboedientes Romano Pontifici, quia Christus plenitudinem potestatis dedit beato Petro pro se et pro locumtenentibus eius.

Item dicis te credere, quod quilibet Pontifex Romanus, qui summus est, praeteritus, praesens et futurus, erat, est et erit locumtenens beati Petri, quia fuit et est et erit immediate universalis Christi Vicarius.

Item promittis, quod quantum in te erit, facere curabis omnes subditos tuos, ecclesiasticos et saeculares, praedicta omnia et singula firmiter credere et tenere.

Super hiis ergo querimus *primo:* si credidisti, credis vel credere es paratus cum Ecclesia Armenorum quae tibi oboedit, quod beatus Petrus plenissimam potestatem iurisdictionis acceperit super omnes fideles christianos a Domino Jesu Christo et quod omnis potestas iurisdictionis, quam in certis terris et provinciis et diversis partibus Orbis specialiter et particulariter habuerunt Judas Thadeusac ceteri Apostoli, subiecta fuerit plenissime auctoritati et potestati, quam super quoscunque in Christum credentes in omnibus partibus Orbis beatus Petrus ab ipso Domino Jesu Christo accepit et quod nullus Apostolus vel quicunque alius super omnes christianos, nisi solus Petrus plenissimam potestatem accepit?

Secundo: si credidisti, tenuisti vel credere ac tenere paratus es cum Armenis tibi subiectis, quod omnes Romani Pontifices, qui beato Petro succedentes canonice intraverunt et canonice intrabunt, ipsi beato Petro Romano Pontifici successerint et succedent in eadem plenitudine iurisdictione potestatis, quam ipse beatus Petras accepit a Domino Jesu Christo super totum et universum corpus Ecclesiae militantis?

Tertio: si credidistis et creditis tu et Armeni tibi subiecti, Romanos Pontifices qui fuerunt et Nos qui sumus Pontifex Romanus ac illos qui in posterum successive erunt, tamquam legitimos et potestate plenissimos Christi Vicarios omnem potestativam iurisdictionem quam Christus ut Caput conforme in humana vita habuit, immediate ab ipso Christo super totum ac universum Corpus militantis Ecclesiae accepisse?

Quarto: si credidisti et credis, quod omnes Romani Pontifices qui fuerunt, Nos qui sumus et alii qui erunt in posterum, ex plenitudine potestatis et auctoritatis praemissae, potuerunt, possumus et poterunt immediate per Nos et eos de omnibus tamquam de iurisdictione Nostra ac eorum subditis iudicare et ad iudicandum quoscunque voluerimus ecclesiasticos iudices constituere et delegare?

Quinto: si credidisti et credis, quod in tantum fuerit, sit et erit suprema et praeeminens auctoritas et iuridica potestas Romanorum Pontificum qui fuerunt, Nostri qui sumus et illorum qui in posterum erunt, ut a nemine iudicari potuerint, potuerimus neque in posterum poterunt, sed soli Deo iudicandi servati fuerint, servemur et servabuntur et quod a sententiis et iudiciis Nostris non potuerit neque possit nec poterit ad aliquem iudicem alium appellari?

Sexto: si credidisti et adhuc credis, plenitudinem potestatis Romani Pontificis se extendere in tantum, quod patriarchas, catholicon, archiepiscopos, episcopos, abbates et quoscunque Praelatos alios de dignitatibus in quibus fuerint constituti, possint ad alias dignitates maioris vel minoris iurisdictionis transferre vel exigentibus eorum criminibus, ipsos degradare et deponere, excommunicare et Sathanae tradere?

Septimo: si credidisti et adhuc credis, pontificalem auctoritatem non posse nec debere subici cuicunque imperiali vel regali aut alteri saeculari potestati, quantum ad institutionem iudicialem, correctionem vel destitutionem?

Octavo: si credidisti et credis Romanum Pontificem posse sacros generales canones condere, plenissimam indulgentiam dare visitantibus limina Apostolorum Petri et Pauli vel ad Terram Sanctam accedentibus aut quibuscunque fidelibus vere et plene poenitentibus et confessis?

Nono: si credidisti et credis, omnes qui se contra fidem Romanae Ecclesiae erexerunt et in finali impoenitentia mortui fuerunt, damnatos fuisse et ad perpetua infernorum supplicia descendisse?

Decimo: si credidisti et adhuc credis, Romanum Pontiflcem circa administrationem Sacramentorum Ecclesiae, salvis semper illis quae sunt de integritate et necessitate Sacramentorum, posset diversos ritus Ecclesiarum Christi tolerare et etiam concedere ut serventur?

Undecimo: si credidisti et credis Armenos, qui Romano Pontifici in diversis partibus Orbis oboediunt et formas ac ritus Romanae Ecclesiae in administratione Sacramentorum et in ecclesiasticis officiis, ieiuniis et aliis caerimoniis, studiose et cum devotione observant, bene agere et ita agendo vitam aeternam mereri?

Duodecimo: si credidisti et credis, neminem de dignitate episcopali ad archiepiscopalem, patriarchalem vel catholicon posse transferri auctoritate propria nec etiam auctoritate cuiuscunque principis saecularis, sive rex fuerit sive imperator vel quicunque alius, fultus qualicunque potestate et dignitate terrena?

Tertiodecimo: si credidisti et adhuc credis, solum Romanum Pontificem, dubiis emergentibus circa fidem catholicam, posse per determinationem authenticam, cui sit inviolabiliter adhaerendum, finem imponere et esse verum et catholicum, quidquid ipse auctoritate clavium sibi traditarum a Christo determinat esse verum; et quod determinat esse falsum et haereticum, sit censendum?

Quartodecimo: si credidisti et credis, Novum et Vetus Testamentum in omnibus libris quos Romanae Ecclesiae nobis tradidit auctoritas, veritatem indubiam per omnia continere?

Respondendo vero ad articulos etiam Minoris Armeniae Ecclesiae per Nos missos, praemittis, quod quae dicturus es, sunt de doctrina Veteris et Novi

Testamenti, Thadaei et Bartholomaei Apostolorum et universalis concilii Sanctae, Catholicae et Apostolicae Ecclesiae tradita ut credenda et tenenda Ecclesia Armenorum *et cetera*.

Super quo a te querimus quae sequuntur:

Primo: si credidisti, quod doctrina Novi et Veteris Testamenti a beatis Apostolis Thadeo et Bartholomaeo fuerit edita vel solis illis praedicantibus Ecclesiae Catholicae per eos manifestata?

Secundo: si credidisti et credis Thadeum Judam et Bartholomaeum, Andreae, Jacobo Maiori et Minori, Johanni Evangelistae ac ceteris a Petro Apostolis, praefuisse vel maioris auctoritatis fuisse?

Secundo capitulo scribis, te et Armenos tibi oboedientes credere, quod Spiritus Sanctus procedit a Patre et Filio et quod usque nunc particulariter tu et Armeni tibi oboedientes dixistis, sed deinceps quantum poteris facies hoc generaliter dici. — Circa quod capitulum per te ad sequentia volumus responderi:

Primo: si credidisti et tenuisti, esse de necessitate salutis credere, quod Spiritus Sanctus non a solo Patre, sed etiam a Filio ab aeterno procedit?

Secundo: si illos, qui expresse negabant Spiritum Sanctum a Filio procedere, pro schismaticis et haereticis habuisti, habes et es semper in posterum habiturus?

Tertio: si in officio Missae, diebus, quibus secundum consuetudinem Romanae Ecclesiae cantatur primum Symbolum, es paratus et promptus cantare et coram populo profiteri, quod Spiritus Sanctus a Patre Filioque procedit, prout in dicto Symbolo continetur?

Quarto: si credidisti et credis, Spiritum Sanctum procedere a Patre et Filio tamquam ab uno principio per unam spirationem, communem Patri et Filio existentem, prout docent Romanae Ecclesiae concilium generale et Doctores catholici, quos eadem Ecclesia veneratur ut sanctos?

Quinto: si credidisti et credis, Spiritum Sanctum cum Patre et Filio esse unum Deum et eis per omnia esse aequalem, potestate, voluntate, immensitate ei in omni prefectione; non inferiorem gradu nec tempore posteriorem, sed eadem aeternitate aeternum?

Sexto: quia scribis, quod usque nunc particulariter dixisti Spiritum Sanctum procedere a Patre et Filio, sed deinceps quantum poteris facies generaliter dici. Querimus a te, si per *particulariter* intelligis quod ad partem et non in publico dicebas vel quod aliqui ex Armenis, licet particulares et pauci, credebant et dicebant Spiritum Sanctum procedere a Patre et Filio? *generaliter* tamen Armeniae Minoris comunitas, quod a Filio Spiritus Sanctus procederet, non credebat nec dicebat neque videtur ad dicendum parata faciliter; quia tu scribis, quod quantum poteris facies *generaliter* dici.

Secundo capitulo scribis, te credere et tenere, quod in una sola persona Christi sunt duae naturae: humana scilicet et divina, unitae. — Super quo scire volumus, si credis vel credere es paratus tu et Armeni qui tibi oboediunt, in Christo solam personam aeternam esse Dei filii, in duabus perfectis et integris naturis, divina siquidem quam aeternaliter habuit et humanam, quam ex tempore de virginali utero beatae Mariae matris suae assumpsit?

Secundo: si reputas omnes illos hereticos, qui credunt et credent in futurum, quod in Christo non manet nisi una natura, quemadmodum in eo non est nisi una sola persona et si tu et Armeni qui tibi oboediunt detestamini Eutychen et Dioscorum et ceteros eorum complices haereticos, Christi carnem et divinam essentiam in unam confundentes naturam, vel dicentes Christum nihil maternae substantiae suscepisse, sed tantum Dei naturam sub habitu latere humano, quemadmodum latet homo sub indumento et beatum Leonem, sub quo celebratum est Calcedonense Concilium et praedictam haeresim et dictos haereticos condemnavit, firmiter creditis divinam essentiam inter Sanctos alios clare videre et beatifice ea frui?

Tertio: si credidisti vel credere es paratus, Macharium Antiochenum episcopum et eius complices socios, qui unam voluntatem et operationem adstruebant in Christo, per Romanum Pontiflcem Agathonem in sexta Constantinopolitana Synodo cum eorum haeresi iuste et catholice condemnatos et anathematizatos fuisse?

Quarto: si credidistis et creditis, tu et Armeni qui tibi oboediunt, Vartan quem, prout Nobis a pluribus est relatum et assertum, Armeni pro speciali doctore habuerunt et qui multos de Armenia Minori labe haeresis infecit, docens et scribens, quod Spiritus Sanctus non procedit a Filio, sed a solo Patre et quod Christus non habet nisi unam solam naturam et quod non dedit ipse Christus maiorem potestatem Petro, quam aliis Apostolis et quod Romana Ecclesia non habet iurisdictionem nec aliquam potestatem super Ecclesiam Armenorum et quod spiritus omnium hominum fuerint in simul a Deo creati et quod animae salvandae et damnandae usque ad diem iudicii manent extra Paradisum et extra Infernum nec sanctae animae Deum per essentiam beatifice videbunt neque fruentur eo usque ad diem iudicii; nec illae, quae cum peccato mortali a suis corporibus recesserunt, usque ad praedictam diem finalis iudicii cruciabuntur in Inferno; et quod pro animabus beatae Virginis, beatorum Petri et Pauli Apostolorum et omnium Sanctorum Martyrum et illorum qui decesserunt sine culpa quacunque et absque omni obligatione ad Purgatorii poenas, ab Ecclesia Catholica est orandum; et quod Christus secundum humanitatem est aequalis Deo Patri; sic de multis aliis erroribus, quibus est unus magnus liber, quem dictus Vartan composuisse adversus fidem sanctam Romanae Ecclesiae dicitur, per totum respersus, fuisse haereticum et haeresiarcham pessimum ac ipsum cum dictis haeresibus et aliis quibuscunque in libro illo vel in aliis scripturis aut doctrinis eiusdem contentis, in quantum scripturae illae aut quaecunque eius doctrinae vel dicta, contraria sunt scripturae et doctrinae fidei Jesu Christi, quam Romana docet et tenet Ecclesia; et omnia Armenorum concilia ubicunque et per quoscunque fuerint congregata contra fidem Romanae Ecclesiae et articulos fidei christianae, quos docet et tenet Romana Ecclesia, reputatis, creditis et tenetis fuisse congregationem haereticorum et adversariorum fidei domini nostri Jesu Christi et si eos, qui talia docuerunt, haereticos et eorum doctrinam ut haereticam anathematizatis et detestamini ut fidei Jesu Christi venenum?

III. In *tertio capitulo* dicis, vos credere, quod nati et nascituri ex viro et muliere, contrahunt originale peccatum, praeter peccata personalia, quae primi parentes, comedendo de fructu ligni vetito contra praeceptum eis datum a Domino, contraxerunt. — Circa quod capitulum a te et ab Armenis qui tibi oboediunt scire volumus:

Primo: si creditis, quod actualia primorum parentum peccata nati et nascituri ex eis contraxerunt et contrahent in futurum, quemadmodum ab ipsis contrahunt originale peccatum?

Secundo: si creditis, quod propter omnia actualia peccata primorum parentum contrahatur originale peccatum?

Tertio: si creditis, quod circa aperitionem regni caelorum, tantum operaretur circumcisio ante institutionem Baptismi et omnium per propagationem a primis parentibus descendentium in utroque sexu obligationem ad ipsam, quantum ex tune operatur Baptismus?

VI. *Sexto capitulo* dicis te cum Armenis tibi oboedientibus credere, quod omnes animae defunctorum ex toto purgatae a peccatis post passionem Christi statim vadunt ad regnum caelorum, ubi Deum manifeste vident; et animae decedentium in peccato mortali vadunt in Infernum damnationis, ubi nunquam Deum videbunt, sed sensuali pugnitione (sic!) ibidem puniuntur. — Circa quod scire volumus a te.

Primo: si credis vel credere es paratus, quod post passionem et ascensionem Domini Jesu Christi animae eorum qui decesserunt in Christi gratia et in quibus nihil fuit purgabile quando decesserunt, ascendant in caelorum regnum et paradisum caelestem et cum Christo et sanctorum angelorum consortio congregatae, divinam essentiam videant visione faciali sicut est, ipsa divina essentia se immediate, clare et aperte eis ostendente?

Secundo: si credidisti vel credere es paratus, quod eadem fruantur essentia animae nihil habentes purgabile a suis corporibus separatae et quod ex visione et fruitione divinae essentiae sint vere beatae et quod huiusmodi intuitiva et facialis clara et aperta visio et fruitio in eisdem animabus sine aliqua intercisione seu evacuatione continuata existit et continuabitur usque ad finale iudicium et extunc usque in sempiternum?

Tertio: si credis vel credere es paratus, quod animae decedentium in actuali mortali peccato mox post mortem suam ad inferna descendunt, ubi poenis infernalibus cruciantur sine remedio et sine extinctione ignis, cum perpetua poena carentiae visionis et fruitionis beatae?

VII. *Septimo capitulo* dicis, te cum Armenis tibi oboedientibus credere, quod vera felicitas stat in visione Dei et non in visione alicuius alterius rei. — Circa quod volumus a te scire:

Primo: si credidisti et credis, quod vera felicitas non consistit in visione Dei per speculum in enigmate, sed in visione qua facie ad faciem Deus sicut est videtur?

Secundo: si credidisti et credis quod vera felicitas sine dilatione correspondente (?) faciali Dei visioni non habetur?

VIII. Circa *octavum capitulum* quaerimus:

Primo: si credidisti et credis, quod Christus secundum humanitatem non excedit infinita perfectione omnem creaturam nec beatitudo creata, qua eius anima est beata, infinita perfectione excedit beatitudinem angelorum vel beatarum animarum?

Secundo: si credidisti et credis, Christum secundum humanitatem, qua minor est Patre, excedi in infinitum et sine termino a perfectione quam habet secundum divinitatem, in qua Patri et Sancto Spiritui est aequalis?

X. Circa *decimum capitulum* quaerimus, si credidisti et credis Purgatorium esse, ad quod descendunt animae decedentium in gratia, quae nondum per completam poenitentiam de suis satisfecerunt peccatis? — Item si credidisti et credis, quod igne crucientur ad tempus et quod mox purgatae etiam citra diem iudicii ad veram et aeternam beatitudinem perveniant, quae in faciali Dei visione et dilectione consistit?

In *XII capitulo* dicis, quod Baptismus secundum formam Ecclesiae receptus sine simulatione, delet omnia peccata illorum qui semel baptizantur, sive originalia sint sive actualia; sed cum aliqui baptizantur bis in eodem Baptismo, non delentur peccata illorum, imo potius adduntur et committuntur per secundum Baptismum. — Circa quod:

Primo: volumus a te scire, si credis, quod Baptismus susceptus secundum formam Romanae Ecclesiae quae est: *Ego te baptizo in nomine Patris et Filii et Spiritus Sancti,* in illis, qui non simulate nec flete suscipiunt, deleat omnia originalia et actualia, si insunt illis, peccata?

Secundo: si credis praedictam formam qua Romana Ecclesia utitur, Christum instituisse et tradidisse Apostolis et ipsam a Christo et per Apostolos fuisse impositam Catholicae Ecclesiae, quae Romana est, ad servandum?

Tertio: si credis, quod a quocunque mortali homine habente fidem Sacramenti, etiam non sacerdote vel clerico, sed laico vel mullere, Baptismus conferatur in forma qua utitur Romana Ecclesia, verum Baptisma esse nec posse scienter iterari ab aliquo ministro nec suscipi ab illo, qui in dicta forma Romanae Ecclesiae semel fuerit baptizatus, sine mortali peccato?

Quarto: si credis, posito quod licitum esset inter prolationem verborum formae Baptismi et lotionem cum aqua baptismali evangelium vel aliquas orationes interponere, quod multo melius et magis ordinate fiat si, quando proferuntur verba Baptismi, lotio simul fiat cum aqua baptismali illius qui baptizatur?

Quinto: si credis nulla auctoritate cui a Catholico sit adhaerendum aut efficaci ratione posse probari, quod forma qua utitur Romana Ecclesia baptizando, sit dubia et incerta et quod Apostoli ea usi non fuerint baptizantes? — Quod pro tanto a te scire volumus, quia misisti quasdam rationes debiliter concludentes, pro eo quam maxime quod supponis in omnibus illis rationibus, quae deberes probare.

Circa *XVII capitulum,* in quo dicis te credere, quod Matrimonium est Sacramentum Ecclesiae et quod actus matrimonialis, si congruo modo fiat, est meritorius, volumus a te scire, si credis Matrimonii Sacramentum perfectum et per carnalem copulam consummatum nequaquam posse dissolvi quantum ad vinculum aliter quam per mortem alterius coniugis vel amborum, dicente Domino: *Quos Deus coniunxit, homo non separet? Secundo:* si credis, quod uxore mortua, qui fuit vir eius possit nubere cum secunda et, illa mortua, cum tertia et sic deinceps, quamdiu placuerit sibi et fuerit coniugio aptus; et quod simili modo uxor, suo primo viro mortuo, possit secundo nubere et, tertio mortuo, similiter, et sic de aliis mortuis viris primis?

Circa *XXIII capitulum,* in quo dicis te credere, quod natura humana assumpta a Verbo est substantialiter unita Verbo in unitate personae, quaerimus a te, si credis unitatem naturae humanae et divinae in Verbo non esse substantialem, sed personalem; nec naturas divinam et humanam unitas esse substantialiter, sed suppositaliter in unitate personae?

Circa *XXIV capitulum,* in quo dicis et promittis, quod curabis facere, ut subditi tui non recipiant manuum impositionem nisi ab hiis qui oboediunt tibi, sicut et tu Ecclesiae Romanae, quaerimus:

Primo: a te, si credis, quod illi qui Romanae Ecclesiae et tibi oboediunt, a Romano Pontifice vel ab aliis episcopis auctoritate Romani Pontificis possunt recipere manuum impositionem?

Secundo: si credis, quod omnes qui tibi oboediunt, teneantur immediatius et principalius quam tibi, Romano Pontifici oboedire?

Circa *XXX et XXXI capitula,* in quibus dicis, *primo,* quod carnes animalium, quae occiduntur pro sepulturis defunctorum, ut adiuventur per eleemosynas et quod distinctio de mundis et immundis animalibus, quantum ad esum, quae praecipiebantur in Lege Veteri, cessavit et evacuata est per adventum Christi; — quaerimus a te, si credis, quod huiusmodi eleemosynae, quae fiunt de carnibus prohibitis in Lege, prosint animabus defunctorum plus quam si fierent de non prohibitis? et quam proficerent eis, si de pane, vino vel panno seu rebus aliis, quibus sacerdotes et alii pauperes tantum vel amplius indigerent?

Circa *XXXII capitulum,* in quo scribis, non esse de consuetudine Armenorum pisces et oleum comedere in diebus ieiuniorum, imo per mandatum Ecclesiae Armenorum prohibitum est comedere pisces et oleum et quod laudatis illos qui una comestione contenti sunt in diebus ieiuniorum, quaerimus:

Primo: a te, si credis, non esse mandatum Ecclesiae Catholicae, quod in diebus ieiuniorum omnes ieiunantes abstineant piscibus et oleo nec quod talis abstinentia sit de necessitate ieiunii a Sanctis Patribus instituti?

Secundo: si credis, quod qui pluribus vicibus in die quam una comedunt, violant ieiunium a Romana Ecclesia et Sanctis Patribus institutum?

In *capitulo XXXIX* dicis, quod rite baptizati in Ecclesia catholica et apostolica nullo modo sunt iterum baptizandi. Circa quod quaerimus a te, si per Ecclesiam catholicam et apostolicam intelligis Ecclesiam Romanam?

Secundo: si in Symbolo ubi nos habemus: *in unam sanctam catholicam,* ut et Armeni qui tibi oboediunt habetis: *Et in hanc sanctam Catholicam* et si estis parati dicere: *Et in unam,* ut Romana Ecclesia dicit?

In *XLII capitulo* dicis, te credere et tenere, quod Corpus Christi natum de Virgine et mortuum in Cruce, quod nunc est in caelo vivum, post verba consecrationis panis quae sunt: *Hoc est corpus meum,* est in Sacramento altaris sub specie et similitudine panis; ex quo quaerimus a te:

Primo: si credis, quod panis transubstantietur in Corpus Christi?

Secundo: si post illa verba: *Hoc est corpus meum,* sacerdotes in Ecclesia Armenorum utuntur orationibus, per quos videantur orare, quod panis convertatur et transeat in corpus Christi vel quod fiat in corpus Christi? et si huiusmodi orationes es tu et Armeni qui tibi oboediunt paratus omnino et ex toto dimittere vel saltem corrigere quantum ad hoc, quod optando oratur, ut corpus Christi fiat in altari, postquam per verba consecrationis vere et realiter in ipso Sacramento est Corpus Christi?

Tertio: quaerimus a te, quibus verbis utuntur sacerdotes Armenorum in consecratione sanguinis Jesu Christi?

Et pro conclusione eorum quae scripsisti in capitulis LIII, volumus a te scire, si omnia scripta per te submittis correctioni nostrae, tamquam veri Vicarii Jesu Christi et successoris beati Petri principis Apostolorum in plenissima potestate super omnes qui invocant nomen Domini nostri Jesu Christi? et correctioni etiam successorum nostrorum ac Romanae Ecclesiae, quae nunquam potest deficere in credendis?

Rursus circa responsiones tuas ad instructiones datas tibi et Armenis qui tibi oboediunt, per saepedictos Johannem archiepiscopum et Antonium episcopum, responsiones dedisti, quae *Nos* inducunt, ut a te sequentia requiramus:

Primo: de consecratione Chrismatis, si credis, quod per nullum sacerdotem, qui non est episcopus, Chrisma potest rite et debite consecrari?

Secundo: si credis, quod Sacramentum Confirmationis per alium quam per episcopum non potest ex officio ordinarie ministrari?

Tertio: si credis, quod solum per Romanum Pontificem, plenitudinem potestatis habentem, possit dispensatio Sacramenti Confirmationis presbyteris, qui non sunt episcopi, committi?

Quarto: si credis, quod chrismati per quoscunque sacerdotes qui non sunt episcopi, neque a Romano Pontifice super hoc commissionem seu concessionem aliquam receperunt, iterum per episcopum vel episcopos sint chrismandi?

Circa instructionem secundam, quod parvulis, quando baptizantur, non debet dari corpus Christi nec poni in ore eorum, respondes, quod dabitur solummodo illis, qui in aetate adulta baptizantur. — Circa quam responsionem quaerimus, si credis, quod ante usum rationis nulli ministranda sit hostia consecrata?

Secundo: si aetatem adultam, in qua nullus sit idoneus recipere Corpus et Sanguinem Jesu Christi, non credis usque quo saltem compleverit septimum annum?

Circa quartam instructionem, in qua agitur de Sacramento Extremae-Unctionis, si credis, quod omnis homo mortalis adultus in eo solo casu quo graviter est infirmus et in mortali periculo constitutus, debet devote et fideliter, semel dumtaxat in eadem infirmitate, Sacramentum Extremae-Unctionis requirere et suscipere? quod si, non habens fidem huiusmodi Sacramento, omitteret, vel sacerdos ex eadem causa administrare nollet, peccarent ambo graviter et errarent in fide?

Circa instructionem nonam, quae erat quod Armenis qui rationabiliter dubitabunt, utrum veraciter in forma qua Armeni baptizant fuerint baptizati, non prohibeantur baptizari secundum formam Ecclesiae Romanae conditionaliter, respondisti, quod rite baptizati in Ecclesia Armenorum, a quocunque baptizantur, nullo modo iterato baptizandi sunt; sed qui dubitabunt rationabiliter, debent dubitationem suam deferre ad sapientes

Praelatos Ecclesiae Armenorum, qui, si opus fuerit, baptizabunt eos secundum formam Armenorum. Circa quam responsionem:

Primo: quaerimus a te, in casu quo baptizati in forma Armenorum dubitarent an esserit baptizati vel non et pro dubitatione amputanda de cordibus eorum ad Romanam Ecclesiam recurrerent, si paratus es credere verum esse quod Romana determinaret Ecclesia?

Secundo: si Armeni dubitantes de forma Baptismi in qua baptizat Ecclesia Armenorum, ad sapientes Praelatos Ecclesiae Armenorum suam dubitationem deferrent, volumus a te scire, utrum tales benigne et caritative susciperent et dubitationi eorum per Sacrae Scripturae instructionem satisfacerent, vel potius dubios flagellarent, incarcerarent et occiderent, sicut Nobis relatum est quod fecerunt de illis Armenis, qui secundum formam Romanae Ecclesiae per dictos nostros nuntios sub conditione baptizati fuerunt?

Circa instructionem XI, quae est, ut Armeni festivitates celebrent in diebus per Romanam Ecclesiam institutis, respondes, quod capitales festivitates ita celebratis sicut Romana Ecclesia, alias autem festivitates celebratis secundum kalendarium Armenorum. — Circa quam responsionem quaerimus, si es paratus tu et Armeni tibi subditi, celebrare festivitates Sanctorum, quos honorat et veneratur ubique Romana Ecclesia? et si kalendarium quo utitur Romana ecclesia estis parati recipere, ut utamini eo in venerando et honorando Sanctos, quos veneratur et honorat Romana Ecclesia diebus ad hoc per Romanam Ecclesiam institutis?

In sextadecima instructione respondes, quod illos Sanctos, quos catholica et apostolica Ecclesia iam acceptavit et honoravit, tu et Armeni acceptatis et honoratis similiter; et Sanctos, quos acceptat et honorat Ecclesia Romana, acceptatis et honoratis et de cetero, cum acceptabitis et honorabitis sicut sanctum, facietis de voluntate et scitu Ecclesiae Romanae.

Circa quam responsionem, *primo*, quaerimus a te, si credis catholicam et apostolicam Ecclesiam esse eandem vel aliam quam Romanam Ecclesiam? quod pro tanto cogimur quaerere, quia in responsione immediate praemissa, sanctam, catholicam Ecclesiam videris distinguere a Romana, ac si crederes Ecclesiam Romanam non esse catholicam.

Secundo: si credis haereticos et haeresiarchas, sicut dicuntur fuisse Dioscorus, Eriscartus, Jacobus et Rassuset plures alii, non esse per Ecclesiam Catholicam honorandos et venerandos ut Sanctos, sed potius anathematizandos et detestandos?

Circa instructionem XIX de illegitime natis, quod non promoveantur ad Sacros Ordines sine dispensatione Romani Pontificis, respondes, quod Catholicon Armenorum usque nunc dispensavit et vis quod de cetero ita fiat, quamvis raro cum talibus dispensetur.

Circa quam responsionem volumus a te scire, cum dispensatio illegitime natis ut ad Sacros Ordines valeant promoveri, sit casus inter alios specialiter Romano Pontifici reservatus, sicut vis, ut ceteri episcopi oboedientes Romano Pontifici in praedicto casu non possint dispensare sine speciali privilegio et concessione Pontificis Romani?

Circa instructionem XX, quae est de libris, quibus utitur Ecclesia Armenorum, respondes, quod in illis non sunt errores, sed laudes et gloria Dei; et in quibus necesse esset eos corrigere, corrigerentur.

Circa quam responsionem quaerimus a te, quare libros, quibus in officiis Missarum et horarum et ordinationum et consecrationum episcoporum utitur Ecclesia Armenorum, non exhibuisti nec etiam ad legendum exhibere voluisti interpreti archiepiscopi et episcopi praedictorum?

Secundo: volumus a te scire, si fideliter et integre es paratus eos exhibere nostris nuntiis, cum per eos fueris requisitus?

Tertio: tu non respondes de libris illorum, quos apud Armenos reputas doctores, in quibus, ut Nobis relatum est, sunt multi errores et haereses contra eandem fidem catholicam, quam tenet et docet sancta mater Ecclesia. — Volumus igitur a te scire, si es paratus ad mandatum nostrum, quando ad te pervenerit, libros huiusmodi exhibere?

Post praedicta omnia mirari cogimur vehementer, quod in quadam epistola, quae incipit *Honorabilibus in Christo Patribus* subtrahis de LIII primis capitulis capitula XVI: *Primum,* quod Spiritus Sanctus procedit a Patre et Filio. *Tertium,* quod parvuli ex primis parentibus contrahunt originale peccatum. *Sextum,* quod animae ex toto purgatae, separatae a suis corporibus, manifeste Deum vident. *Nonum,* quod animae decedentium in mortali peccato in Infernum descendant. *Duodecimum,* quod baptismus deleat originale et actuale peccatum. *Decimumtertium,* quod Christus non destruxit, descendendo ad inferos, inferiorem Infernum. *Quintumdecimum,* quod angeli fuerunt creati boni. *Trigesimum,* quod effusio sanguinis animalium nullam operatur remissionem peccatorum. *Trigesimum secundum,* quod non iudicent comestores piscium et olei in diebus ieiuniorum. *Trigesimum nonum,* quod in Ecclesia Catholica baptizati, si efficiantur infideles et postmodum convertantur, non sunt iterum baptizandi. *Quadragesimum,* quod parvuli ante octavum diem possunt baptizari et quod Baptismus non potest esse in liquore alio quam in vera aqua. *Quadragesimum secundum,* quod corpus Christi post verba consecrationis sit idem numero quod corpus natum de Virgine et immolatum in cruce. *Quadragesimum quintum,* quod nullus, etiam Sanctus, corpus Christi potest conficere, nisi sit sacerdos. *Quadragesimum sextum,* quod est de necessitate salutis confiteri proprio sacerdoti vel de licentia eius, omnia peccata mortalia perfecte et distincte.

Quia igitur verba illius epistolae in qua scribis, quod diminuisti XVI capitula de LIII capitulis per dictos archiepiscopum et episcopum tibi exhibitxs et ad singula per te illis in scriptis responsionibus datis intricata sunt et obscura, ideo volumus clare et sine velamine a te scire, si praedicta XVI capitula diminuisti de LIII pro eo quod non credis ea esse vera neque catholica vel ex qua causa ipsa capitula diminuisti?

Item, in scriptis rogasti archiepiscopum et episcopum antefatos, ut essent inter eos et te verborum finis; et quod amplius non laboreretis in verbis instructionis, ad quem laborem iidem archiepiscopus et episcopus per Romanam Sedem fuerant ad te missi. Et cum tuae responsiones in pluribus sint dubiae, cavillosae, obscurae et suspectae, scias, quod non possemus Nos, qui salutem tuam et Armenorum, sicut tenemur, ardenti desiderio sitimus, finem imponere nec a labore et fatigatione cessare, nisi prius pure, clare, perfecte et integre tu et Armeni de tua oboedientia fidem illam receperitis, quam ipsa Romana tenet et docet Ecclesia, quae cunctorum fidelium mater est et magistra.

Adhuc, cum canonisationes Sanctorum et promotiones illegitimorum ad Sacros Ordines sint casus, qui inter alios tantummodo Romano Pontifici reservantur et ad nullum alium Praelatum Ecclesiae pertinentes, nisi ipse Romanus Pontifex specialiter aliquibus duxerit committendos, miramur, quod tu dicis praedictos duos casus auctoritate propria velle penes te retinere; quod nullum signum est oboedientiae et reverentiae, quas ad Romanum Pontificem in praemissis capitulis te praetendis habere. Quapropter adhuc cogimur te requirere, ut Nobis in scriptis respondeas, si vis traditiones orthodoxorum Patrum ac Decretales seu Constitutiones sanctae et apostolicae Romanae Sedis reverenter suscipere, docere atque servare?

Ceterum, quia fide dignorum plurium et quorundam etiam Armenorum relatio frequenter nostris auribus instillavit, quod tu et antecessores tui Catholicon Armenorum ac tibi et eis oboedientes Armeni, ea quae circa ipsius fidei nostrae cultum Nobis et praedecessoribus nostris Romanis Pontificibus, tuis et eorum litteris descripsistis et promisistis etiam vos facturos, in nullo penitus observatis, imo, quod est detestabilius et Nos amplius deploramus, nuntiorum et Legatorum dictae Sedis, quos ad te ac illos Sedes ipsa, de tua et illorum salute anxia, curiositate sollicita destinavit, salubria et sanam catholicamque doctrinam, per eosdem Legatos et nuntios tibi et tuis antecessoribus ac oboedientibus tibi et eis Armenis eisdem communicata et tradita contempsistis et abiecistis omnino ac fidem ipsius Ecclesiae Romanae, extra quam nulli est gratia, nulli salus, habuistis damnabiliter in derisum.

Et ideo fraternitatem tuam monemus, requirimus et hortamur attente, tibi tuae salutis intuitu sanis consiliis suadentes, quatenus responsiones per te ad interrogationes nostras faciendas et omnia quae tu et iidem oboedientes tibi, ut praefertur, Armeni circa ipsius fidei nostrae negotium promittetis et dicetis, vos credere et tenere, quamquam speremus indubie, quod Simplicia verba tua et Armenorum ipsorum pura et vera tua et eorum conscientia, quidquid illi vel illi conentur asserere, comitetur, tactis sacrosanctis Evangeliis, iuramentis solemnibus roboretis et nihilominus sub iuramentis similibus promittatis, quod Nobis et successoribus nostris Romanis Pontificibus canonice intrantibus et eidem Ecclesiae Romanae ac nostris et eorum praeceptis et iussionibus, sicut vere oboedientes, parebitis cum effectu, ut ora de te et Armenis eisdem sic graviter sicque notabiliter obloquentium obstruas et Armeniae cleri et populi pastor bonus sic eis salutis ducatum et pascua praepares, quod dum tempus resolutionis advenerit, ad sancta sanctorum purificatis cum ipsis introire mentibus merearis Nosque laborum nostrorum, quos cum tanta cordis affectione ac sinceritate subivimus et subimus, fructus utiles et diu ac anxie concupitos, praestante Domino nostro Jesu Christo, qui est caput Ecclesiae, colligamus, sciturus pro certo, quod praeter salutis aeternae praemia et famae titulos, quae provide consequeris, dabit tibi Deus, ille omnium opulentissimus retributor, unde in praesenti quoque saeculo gratiis et beneficiis affluas et Nos, licet insufficientibus meritis, dignatione sua eius in terris Vicarius, qui honori et statui Ecclesiae Sedisque suae non detrahere, quinimo adiicere tuis, ut speramus, exigentibus meritis, Deo favente, proponimus, magnis et amplioribus privilegiis, gratiis et libertatibus te ac ipsam tuam Ecclesiam honorare.

Datum apud Villamnovam, Avinionensis diocesis, III kalendas octobris, anno decimo.

The Scriptorium Project is the work of a small group of lay people of various apostolic churches who are interested in the preservation, transmission, and translation of the works of the early and medieval church. Our efforts are to make the works of the church fathers accessible to anyone who might have an interest in Christian antiquities and the theological, philosophical, and moral writings that have become the bedrock of Western Civilization.

To-date, our releases have pulled from the Greek, Syriac, Georgian, Latin, Celtic, Ethiopian, and Coptic traditions of Christianity, and have been pulled from sundry local traditions and languages.

Other Selections from the Armenian Church Series:

Refutations by Eznik of Kolb (Dec. 2007)

Explanation of the Faith of the Armenian Church by Nerses IV the Gracious, Catholicos of Armenia (July 2009)

Super Quibusdam by Pope Clement VI (Nov. 2009)

The Life of Mashtots by Koriun the Iberian (Nov. 2012)

Letter to Kiwron, Catholicos of Iberia by Movses II, Catholic of Armenia (Nov. 2013)

Canons of the Synod of Partav by Sion I, Catholicos of Armenia (Dec. 2013)

The History of the Holy Cross of Aparank by St. Gregory of Narek (Feb. 2014)

Armenian Synaxarium: Volume I- Month of Navasard (Oct. 2018)

The Geography by Ananias of Shirak (Dec. 2020)

Genealogy of the Family of St. Gregory by St. Mesrop Mashtots (Nov. 2023)

www.ingramcontent.com/pod-product-compliance
Lightning Source LLC
LaVergne TN
LVHW061042070526
838201LV00073B/5143